Endorsements

Sheldon Clark conveys an understanding of scripture and of matters spiritual. His gift for composition illuminates *Logos for the Journey* by using historical Quaker references. Sheldon's reflections demand some intense concentration. He challenges one to delve into one's own soul. This collection of quotations, stories, and prayers is not a quick read. It is, however, a thoughtful journey to be undertaken with an open and receptive heart, and afterward to be pondered with appreciation.

—Janice d'Eon, McMaster University (Certificate in Creative Writing), 2004
Insurance Representative in Operations at Travelers Canada (Retired, 2023)
Publications by Janice d'Eon with illustrations by Melissa Rainford:
Annabelle-Lee (2015), *A Perfect Place* (2013),
Feeling Better (2012), *My Wonderful Zoo* (2011)

Sheldon Clark has invited us to travel on a journey of the soul. Enter the quiet capsule of your mind and peer into the darkness for the faint light ahead, to ever-increasing brightness. The scriptures, prayers, and stories we travel are for each to make part of their personal passage, being universal in appeal. Sheldon's work expands the horizon of our collective imagination to our beginning and ending in the Divine Spirit.

—Kathryn Wiersma
McMaster University, Honours B.A. (Kinesiology), 2001
Mohawk College (Early Childhood Education Diploma), 2022

In *Logos for the Journey*, Sheldon Clark has provided us with an important tool to add to our carryalls through life, a thematic collection of scripture, spiritual thoughts, and guidance with a Quaker focus that also transcends specific theological traditions. We are all on a journey, we need all the tools we can get. Especially in the dark days, we are reminded we hold inside ourselves darkness and light, and our inner Peace requires ongoing thoughtful attention.

—Jennifer Preston, McMaster University, Honours B.A. (Anthropology and Dramatic Arts), 1989
University of Guelph, M.A. (Drama), 1990
General Secretary, Canadian Friends Service Committee,
Canadian Yearly Meeting of the Religious Society of Friends

I read *Logos for the Journey* several times and I think it is brilliant. It is a thought-provoking collage/collection of poetry, imagery, and teachings from the ages and the world. It must have been a challenge to assemble. *Logos for the Journey* deserves to be in the hands of every Quaker. Thank you.

—Donald W. Woodside, M.D. (1941–2023)
University of Toronto School of Medicine, 1965

Logos for the Journey is a collection of fifteen thought-provoking reflections. Beware! In the manner of the monastic practice of *Lectio Devina*, readers may experience the presence of the Holy One and be drawn to act as the Holy Spirit leads. Gratitude to Sheldon H. Clark for this helpful compendium for daily living.

—Paul R. Dekar, Ph.D.
Current Co-chair of the Christian Interfaith Reference Group
of the Canadian Council of Churches and
Chair of the Peace and Social Action Committee of Hamilton Friends
Dekar is the author of several books including, in 2022, *Journeying with Hope into a New Year: Reflections for Advent and Christmas*

Logos for the Journey

Sheldon H. Clark

PREVIOUS PUBLICATIONS BY SHELDON H. CLARK

Water Voices (with Amber C. McPhail), 2023
Fire Voices (with Amber C. McPhail), 2022
After the Fire A Still Small Voice (with Catherine Farquhar), 2022
Still Voices (with Ed VandenDool), 2021
Voices Extended (with Neil Paul), 2016 and 2021
Poetry and Prayer Sketches (with George S. Keltika), 2008, 2013, and 2021

Published by
Rock's Mills Press
www.rocksmillspress.com
Oakville, Ontario, Canada

Copyright © 2024 by Sheldon H. Clark.
All rights reserved.

For information, including orders, contact us at:
customer.service@rocksmillspress.com

Whatsoever

Finally, brethren, whatsoever things are true,
whatsoever things are honest,
whatsoever things are just,
whatsoever things are pure,
whatsoever things are lovely,
whatsoever things are of good report;
if there be any virtue, and if there be any praise,
think on these things.
Those things which ye have both learned,
And received, and heard,
And seen in me, do:
And the God of peace shall be with you.

Philippians 4:8

Contents

Endorsements	1
Whatsoever	5
Acknowledgements	7
Introduction	9
ALPHA	11
I. Eternity	12
II. Kindness	14
III. Temptation	16
IV. Spirit	18
V. Forgiveness	20
PRACTICING THE PRESENCE	23
VI. Witness	24
VII. Inasmuch	26
VIII. Worship	28
IX. Sacredness	30
X. Agape	32
OMEGA	35
XI. Acceptance	36
XII. Authority	38
XIII. Moral Development	40
XIV. Evangelizing	42
XV. Renewal	44
Afterword	46
Endnotes	47
Bibliography	49
Electronic	49
Texts	50

Acknowledgments

Many people, places, causes, consequences, rationalizations, and changes in direction have contributed to these meditations, anecdotes, and readings. Each scriptural reference, fragment, commentary, personal reflection, and prayer was written with a conscious awareness that I have traveled with a proverbial knapsack to experience life, "play my part," pray forward my observations, record impressions, overcome obstacles, and learn to choose more wisely. I am keenly aware of the gratitude I owe. I am here because other sojourners opened opportunities. My memory holdall is filled with gratitude.

Individuals

Jared Clark and Margery Clark (1945–2020), Joan A. Clark (1931–2015), Joan Culver, the Honourable G. William Dandie (1931–2024), Paul R. Dekar, Ph.D., Janice d'Eon, Thomas D. Hamm, Ph.D., John Horvath (1945–2020) and Barbara Horvath, Ryan, Fox, and Amber McPhail, Rev. Dr. F. Gardner Perry, Jennifer Preston, Dick and Betty Preston, David and Christine Richardson, Jane Robertson, Beverly Shepard, Kathryn Wiersma, Don and Harriet Woodside, Jane MacKay Wright, and teachers, mentors, and friends whose memories are vividly alive.

Quaker Meetings

Columbus, Ohio, Cleveland, Ohio (Recorded at birth)	1941–1943
Cleveland Meeting, Cleveland, Ohio (Member)	1944–1968
Westtown Friends School, Westtown, Pennsylvania	1956–1959
Weekend Workcamp with David Ritchie, Philadelphia, Pennsylvania	Spring 1959
Pendle Hill, Media, Pennsylvania (AFSC-VISA volunteer)	Summer 1964
Bangalore (South India) Friends Worship Group	1964–1966
Euston Road Friends House, London, England (Visitor)	Summers 1952 & 1966
Woodbrook Quaker Study Centre, Selly Oak, Birmingham, England (Visitor)	Summer 1966
Toronto Friends Meeting, Ontario (Member)	1968–1973
Pickering College, Newmarket, Ontario (Teacher & then Head of School)	1972–1995
Yonge Street Monthly Meeting, Newmarket, Ontario (Member)	1973–2023
Earlham School of Religion Meeting for Worship	1996–2000
Earlham College Friends Meeting, Richmond, Indiana (Visit)	1996–2001
Williamsburg Friends Church, Williamsburg, Indiana (Part-time Pastor)	1997–2000
Indiana Yearly Meeting, Recorded Minister	2000

First Friends, Richmond, Indiana (Attender)	1997–2000
First Friends, New Castle, Indiana (Full-time Pastor)	2001–1004
Indiana Yearly Meeting (Recorded Minister, 2000)	2005—present
Hamilton Friends Meeting, Ontario (Sojourning Member, Member)	2008–2022, 2023–present

Advice

Friends, please observe the five-point pattern developed to aid in the contemplation of this material: subtitles, scripture, Quaker quotation, personal reflection, and prayer. Authorship, other than my own, is duly noted and referenced. Collectively, we inspire each other to witness the stirrings of the Spirit in each other's lives as we travel on our respective spiritual journeys. With the founder of Quakerism, George Fox (1624–1691), we do well to ask, ***"What canst thou say?"***

Introduction

Thematic unity of subject, selected scripture, Quaker quotations, sympathetic thoughts, and personal reflections are united by metaphor. One might consider this eclectic collection an all-purpose carryall into which necessities, whatnots, and mementos are placed. This holdall was useful for travel from some dark places to illuminated spaces; from bystander to participant; from doubt to faith; from the secular to the sacred.

One might approach this material as *Lectio Divina*. Each subject deserves calm reflection. The journey involves choices, failures, successes, dead-ends, and possible paths for a new direction. Margaret Fell (1614–1702), the mother of Quakerism, observed: *"We are all thieves; we are all thieves; we have taken the scriptures in words, and know nothing of them in ourselves."*[1] My journey has been transformative. I went from my comfort zone to places I never dreamed of visiting. I found myself wanting sunscreen by the seashore and wearing sunglasses to see the blended horizon of where earth meets sky and sky meets earth from a mountaintop. My kitbag gradually filled. Your holdall will fill, too.

I was a seminary student at the Earlham School of Religion (ESR) in Richmond, Indiana (1996–1999). As part of my field placement in Clinical Pastoral Education (CPE), I found myself as a visiting chaplain in a psychiatric hospital. The first morning I was asked to lead the "Chap Rap" to a dozen patients in a locked ward activity room. "Mr. Clark is with us today." There was no Cross on which to gaze, no religious insignia anywhere, and no audio-visual aids. There was just me standing in front of a group of mentally challenged individuals. A solitary nurse stood posted near the door. "Show no fear," was my first thought, and then, "Ask a question."

"Friends, what would you like to talk about this morning?" Bemused silence followed. I waited. A person in a droll tone said, "Let's go on a trip." Others chimed, "Trip. Let's take a trip." I wrote on the whiteboard, TRIP. Underneath from left to right, I drew an ascending timeline. "What do we need to take?" Various voices offered, "Sandwiches. Water. Backpacks. Band-Aids. Hats. Boots. Matches. Gloves." I printed: START and FINISH. We then boarded our imaginary bus off to the country. Everyone hiked and saw clouds, jet streams, birds and bees, ants, butterflies, and three deer. We crossed a stream on stepping stones holding hands for safety and climbed a rocky grassy knoll. We sat on outcrops, ate sandwiches, and drank water. We crossed a noisy footbridge with much loud stamping of feet to warn the trolls. We even slept on the bus on the way back. Finally, we arrived at FINISH. Someone quietly said, "Thank you, Father." I was startled.

The nurse now seated by the exit smiled. Her charges, "the students", had been engaged, felt safe, and were happy. Time had evaporated into thin air. Actually, from nine to eleven, we shared laughter and found joy. The hospital was forgotten. I felt the internalized power of scripture beyond words, "have love one to another" (John 13:35). For a brief time, we became "as little children" enjoying a field trip together from a dozen shrouded memories of long ago.

Grab your haversack, imagine your journey, and renew in body, mind, and spirit.

ALPHA

I
ETERNITY

Matthew 28:5–6
Fear not ... He is not here: for he is risen.[2]

William Penn, 1644–1718
The truest end of life is to know the life that never ends.[3]

Reflection

The reality of this life and contemplation about the next have been subject to human preoccupation since time immemorial. Some think that "to be" is all there is. One is born, lives, and dies. Death is a mystery. It is *"the undiscovered country from whose bourn no traveler returns, puzzles the will and makes us bear those ills than fly to others we know not of."*[4] Death is a fact of life. One is born, it is believed in the image of God (*Imago Dei*), in the hope to live to reflect God's purpose, is indeed mortal, and then is born into eternal life. These statements reflect St. Paul's enigmatic definition, not of death, but of faith: *"Now faith is the substance of things hoped for, the evidence of things not seen"* (Hebrews 11:1).

Wonder continues.

Prayer

Holy Spirit Divine, be with us.
We die to ourselves to unite with the Eternal.
This moment of Death is known and unknown.
> Death is inevitable.

We know in our bones that Death comes to all.
We feel Death as emptiness in body, mind, and spirit.
No more suffering. No more anguish. No more pain.
> Death is the great Liberator.

Death is but the momentary pause between Tic and Toc.
Death is the silence between what used to be and what is to be.
We mourn. We rejoice. We hesitate We live by Grace.
> Heavenly Spirit, Divine Presence,
> We are grateful for the mystery, *"to know the life that never ends."*

Amen.

II

KINDNESS

Psalm 92:1–2
It is a good thing to give thanks unto the Lord, and to sing praises unto thy name, O most high: To shew forth thy lovingkindness in the morning, and thy faithfulness every night.

Isaac Penington, 1616–1679
Our life is love, peace, and tenderness, and bearing one another, and forgiving one another, and not laying accusations one against another, but praying one for another, and helping one another up with a tender hand.[5]

Reflection

The child said, "I'm ready, please let go." The child and pony walked confidently around the large fenced-in field. They wove in and out of six pylons and passed by eight crossed pole jumps. "May I trot, now?" "Trot on." The child laughed, relaxed, and was delightfully elated by her newfound confidence. Soft hands. Knees in. Heels down. Balanced. Happy pony. "Next time, I want to canter and jump." Amazed parents smiled and hugged each other.

Be kind. "Lend a Hand" and 'Be Prepared" are the Promise and Motto of the Girl Guides. They emphasize the need to be ready and helpful to address any need. Children and adults who take positive initiative find themselves in leadership positions. Servant-leaders are found among families, in neighborhoods, churches, playgrounds, schools, special needs institutions, religious organizations, business enterprises, sports, in clubs, on farms, and in political organizations. Wherever human beings gather in small or large groups, relationships are inevitably formed based on common interests. Civil behavior, codes of conduct, discipline, and even unspoken rules emerge to give people the opportunity to belong and participate, feel accepted, and enjoy each other's company in a common enterprise. All feel empowered to contribute to the group's *raison d'etre*. Individuals may assume different roles, and work according to their gifts, but when called upon, give willingly of their time, treasure, and talent. Co-operative relationships are key for provisioning the common good. Kindness is the key.

Faith in action is the conviction to live as though the *Parousia* has come.

Prayer

Help us Lord to do our part. Put love in every heart.
Make us kind to everyone. Sorry for any wrong we've done.
Amen.

Channing Clark, 1916–2004
(learned as a Boy Scout, circa 1926)

III

TEMPTATION

Matthew 4:1–11

1 Then was Jesus led up of the spirit into the wilderness to be tempted of the devil.
2 And when he had fasted forty days and forty nights, he was afterward an hungred.
3 And when the tempter came to him, he said, If thou be the Son of God, command these stones to be made bread.
4 But he answered and said, "It is written, Man shall not live by bread alone, but by every word that proceedeth out of the mouth of God."
5 Then the devil taketh him up into the holy city, and setteth him on a pinnacle of the temple,
6 And saith unto him, If thou be the son of God, cast thyself down: for it is written, He shall give his angels charge concerning thee: and in their hands they shall bear thee up, lest at any time thou dash thy foot against a stone.
7 Jesus said unto him, "It is written again, Thou shalt not tempt the Lord thy God."
8 Again, the devil taketh him up into an exceeding high mountain, and sheweth him all the kingdoms of the world, and the glory of them;
9 And saith unto him, All these things will I give thee, if thou wilt fall down and worship me.
10 Then saith Jesus unto him, "Get thee hence, Satan: for it is written, Thou shalt worship the Lord thy God, and him only shalt thou serve."
11 Then, the devil leaveth him, and, behold, angels came and ministered unto him.

Francis Howgill, (Quaker activist), 1618–1668
Why *gad* you abroad?[6]

Reflection

Watch and pray, that [we] enter not into temptation: the spirit is indeed willing, but the flesh is weak (Matthew 26:41).

I wanted to kill him. I hated seeing his hypocritical face. My conscience said: "Change your life." I found inner peace by helping others. I learned I could control my temper. Robert Barclay's words first introduced in a Quakerism class at Westtown School percolated into my brain, "*I found the evil weakening in me and the good raised up.*"[7]

Temptations come when least expected and, in many guises. Temptation is a matter of choice. Knowledge and experience are invaluable to helping one make healthy choices. Question: "Does what I am about to think, choose, say, or do, lead to healthy spiritual, physical, psychological, and social well-being?" People who make mistakes in judgment and live in fear are not alone. When faced with temptation, it takes extraordinary courage to choose the right way and request forgiveness.

Prayer

I sought wealth and became possessive. I sought fame and became prideful.
I sought power and became afraid. I shared wealth and found peace.
I suffered pain and found compassion. I became vulnerable and found Love.

IV

SPIRIT

Luke 17:20–21
Behold, the kingdom of God is within you.

George Fox, 1624–1691
And this is the word of the Lord God to you all, and a charge to you all in the presence of the living God: be patterns, be examples in all countries, places, islands, nations, wherever you come, that your carriage and life may preach among all sorts of people, and to them; then you will come to walk cheerfully over the world, answering that of God in everyone.[8]

Reflection

Juan de Yepes Alvarez (1542–1591), better known as St. John of the Cross, and George Fox (1624–1691) kept journals about their spiritual struggles as they sought spiritual enlightenment. Three hundred years later, Mother Teresa (1910–1997) wrote in an unpublished letter: "My God, I have no faith. I dare not utter the words and thoughts that crowd my heart, afraid to uncover them because of the blasphemy. If there be God, please forgive me." Those examples of spiritual struggle were mental, emotional, physical, personal, and spiritual, and not without effect on their families, friends, and co-religious seekers. They emerged from their respective "dark night journeys of the soul," as committed human beings ready to share their newfound truth about God. The outward differences in terms of the historic period, geography, religious affiliation, and social/political differences could not be more striking. The inner similarities of their respective spiritual journeys are equally striking. People in earnest about their search for God encounter doubt as integral to their faith journey. We might say with the parent whose son could not speak, *"Lord, help thou my unbelief"* (Mark 9:24).

Once a prisoner with a smile on his face, asked me, "Did you know that *Jesus Christ* is the most often repeated name in the English language? Think about it." On another occasion, a nurse helped an unsteady elderly patient move from his runaway walker to sit on a nearby bench and regain his sense of equilibrium. She advised, "Breathe slowly, in and out." He did. The afternoon sun shone more brightly as this unintentional accident had been avoided. Thanks be to God.

Prayer
Emma Wilson, Cleveland Friends Meeting, 1948

Dear God, I am a little child,
please help me to do right.
As Jesus made me good and mild,
I want to mind the Light. Amen.

V

FORGIVENESS

Luke 36:37
Be ye therefore merciful, as your Father also is merciful.
Forgive, and ye shall be forgiven.

Beverly Shepard (Hamilton Monthly Meeting, Canadian Yearly Meeting)
As Quakers, we have no formal confession of sins, repentance, and atonement. We acknowledge that we are imperfect seekers, but our recognition of our flaws and failings is, perhaps, somewhat brusque, not something to be dwelled upon. We concentrate on our strengths and virtues, using them to do God's will. This is good, but it is also a great burden. What a relief, what release, what joy! To say, "God, I mess up—I know it. Forgive me," and to know that God does forgive—and loves us with all our imperfections.[9]

Reflection

Seven women in prison garb chatted as they filed into the prison library and sat around the only table. The guard sat down, too. Seated, one asked, *"Pastor, teach us to pray."* I said, *"Pray for your families and for each other."* Their spoken words came from each one, guard included, as they were meant to do. This prayer circle took on a dynamic power greater than the sum of its imperfect human parts. And then, there was silence. These "friends" quietly left our worship time together to return to their cells clearly uplifted.

In Proverbs 16:18, we read, *Pride goeth before destruction, and an haughty spirit before a fall.* This proverb seems to be directed at an individual. Also, it could apply to humanity's herd instinct. Conformity is a form of pride, too. People learn to take pride in their families, schools, religious affiliations, and business life. "We do things this way, not that way," is a common admonishment. Non-conformity is viewed as threatening. Warning: power over others can be destructive. Weaponized pride and narcissistic behavior inhibit another's initiative. We pray, "God forgive us our fear of being found unacceptable. Let us learn to show love to Creation as the Spirit teaches us to do." Idealistic? Prophetic?

Prayer

Heavenly Father,
We pray to be examples of your Spirit.
We pray to be humble, kind, honest,
grateful, self-controlled, patient, diligent, and loving.
Help us share the gifts You gave us so generously with others.
Forgive us when we make mistakes, and
lead us evermore into the Light of Truth.
Amen.

PRACTICING THE PRESENCE

VI

WITNESS

Mathew 26: 39
O my Father, if it be possible, let this cup pass from me: nevertheless not as I will, but as thou wilt.

John Woolman, 1720–1772
The place of prayer is a precious habitation.[10]

Reflection

My oral reading was terrible. My teacher said, "Think and feel what the words mean. Visualize the idea. Speak them in phrases as though to someone you love. The feelings you project will convey your emotional understanding." Practice did not make perfect, but practice helped. I am still learning.

"We are not human beings having a spiritual experience. We are spiritual beings having a human experience." Pierre Teilhard de Chardin (1881–1955) stated this consummate identity. This is a comfort to those of us who have chosen to live as non-conformists. Actually, it is a comfort, too, to those who choose to conform to belief in a transcendent creative force. Creation simply includes everyone and everything. People seek engagement with life and seek Truth by questioning, doubting, and evolving in body, mind, and spirit. Metamorphosis in the physical universe and in human endeavor does not occur in a vacuum and is unstoppable. Imaginative creativity builds upon the experience from the commonplace to the esoteric. Microscopes and telescopes are opposite lenses for observing the natural world. We need both microscopic and macroscopic perspectives. We want our thoughts and prayers, our minds and hearts to bear witness to ever-evolving truth.

Truth is.

Prayer of Muhammad

O God! Increase my Light everywhere.
O God! Grant me Light in my heart,
Light on my tongue, Light in my eyes, Light in my ears,
Light to my right, Light to my left,
Light above me, Light below me,
Light in front of me, Light behind me,
and Light within my self; increase my Light.[11]

The Prophet Muhammad, 570–632

VII

INASMUCH

Matthew 25:40
Inasmuch as ye have done it unto one of the least of these my brethren, ye have done it unto me.

William Dewsbury, 1621–1688
I … joyfully entered prisons as palaces.[12]

Reflection

Prisons are abnormal places. Warehousing people is society's escape plan for dealing with its so-called undesirables. The incarcerated, the dependent (deaf, blind, multi-handicapped, terminal patients), those with mental disabilities, the elderly, and the dying are relegated to specialized facilities. Human warehousing is big business. "There's gold to be found in them thar hills." Whatever happened to the implementation of the thirty articles in the Universal Declaration of Human Rights? To name only two:

ARTICLE I: **Freedom and equality in dignity and rights.** We are all born free. We all have our own thoughts and ideas and we should all be treated the same way.

ARTICLE III: **Right to life, liberty, and security of person**.[13]

Human beings do not abdicate their humanity or their spiritual selves when they commit crimes, are profoundly diseased, highly dependent, or have reached the last stages of life. We, who are healthy, are charged to provide "domestic tranquility" by treating others with respect and compassion.

Elizabeth Fry (1780–1845) wrote in 1827 of her work for prison reform: "Much depends on the spirit in which the visitor enters upon her work. It must be in the spirit, not of judgment, but of mercy. She must not say in her heart *I am more holy than thou,* but rather keep in perpetual remembrance that '*all* have sinned and come short of the Glory of God.'"[14]

Prayer

God, help. Help.
Be with us. Pardon us.
Our lives are dark. Anger howls.
Help us be at peace.
Faith comes so hard.
Amen.

VIII

WORSHIP

John 4:24
God is a Spirit: and they that worship him must worship him in spirit and in truth.

A Meeting of Elders at Balby, 1656
Dearly beloved Friends, these things we do not lay upon you as a rule or form to walk by, but that all, with the measure of the light which is pure and holy, may be guided; and so in the light walking and abiding, these may be fulfilled in the Spirit, not from the letter, for the letter killeth, but the Spirit giveth life.[15]

Reflection

Mary, a non-swimmer, called from twenty feet away from the tidal shoreline, "Help. Help. Help." Undertow had knocked her off her feet. Her son's friend immediately waded to her, righted her position, helped her expel water, and then they stumbled together to the sandy beach, where she regained breath and composure. Mary said, "I felt I was going to drown. God bless you."

Empowerment comes from the Spirit. Petitionary prayer to the Divine is a way of staying focused. The key is listening to the Inner Light. One needs to question, seek direction, and hear whether one's life path is confirmed. Sensitivity, understanding, and compassion are attributes resulting from the continuous process of questing after Truth. *"The fruit of the Spirit is love, joy, peace, longsuffering, gentleness, goodness, faith. meekness, temperance: against such there is no law"* (Galatians 5:22,23).

Our prayer is to open ourselves to the fruit of the Spirit, to be inspired, and to be empowered to serve others.

Prayer
Dorothy Trimble, 1923–2014, Yonge Street Friends Meeting, Newmarket, Ontario

God, my constant companion and source of inner strength,
Thank you, for Your many blessings.
Let my life be guided by Your Love.
May I have the strength, wisdom and courage
to respond to the promptings of the Light within.
May I be sensitive, understanding and compassionate
in my relations with others.
May I seek and find that which is good,
true, beautiful, and joyous.
May I seek the truth, so that Your Will may be done.
Amen.

IX

SACREDNESS

Luke 24:30–31

And it came to pass, as he sat at meat with them, he took bread, and blessed it, and brake, and gave to them. And their eyes were opened, and they knew him; and he vanished out of their sight.

A. Barratt Brown, 1887–1947

The whole of life is sacramental.[16]

Reflection
Ask Not Good Fortune
Elizabeth G. Watson, 1917–2006

Living unafraid is a vastly different thing from dwelling in safety. The last two words have radically changed their meaning. Fearlessness and safety are not at all the same. And the verb has changed too. To dwell means "to reside, to stay as a permanent resident." A dwelling is "a place of residence, a shelter." To live, on the other hand, has half a column of meanings in my dictionary, including "to exist," "to breathe," and also "to experience and enjoy life to the full." And living, as contrasted with dwelling, is a way of life, not a fixed abode. It can mean, among other things, "flowing freely, like water." God did not really promise us that we could "dwell in safety": God promised us that we need not be overcome. Therefore, no longer ask to dwell in safety. Ask not good fortune. Seek not security in intellectual analyses or theological formulas. Ask, rather, to love and to live unafraid. Grant us wisdom, grant us courage, for the living of these days.[17]

Prayer of Moses—The Shema

Hear, O Israel: The Lord is our God is one Lord: And thou shalt love the Lord thy God with all thine heart, and with all thy soul, and with all thy might.
Deuteronomy 6:4–5

Prayer of Jesus—The Great Commandment

Jesus said unto him, Thou shalt love the Lord thy God with all thy heart, and with all thy soul, and with all thy mind. This is the first and great commandment. And the second is like unto it, Thou shalt love your neighbour as thyself. On these two commandments hang all the law and the prophets.
Matthew 22: 37–40

X

AGAPE

Luke 11:1
And it came to pass, that, as he was praying in a certain place, when he ceased, one of his disciples said unto him, Lord, teach us to pray, as John also taught his disciples.

Luke 23:34
Father, forgive them; for they know not what they are doing.

James Nayler, 1660
There is a spirit which I feel that delights to do no evil, nor to revenge any wrong, but delights to endure all things, in hope to enjoy its own in the end. Its hope is to outlive all contention and to weary out all exaltation and cruelty, or whatever is of a nature contrary to itself. It sees to the end of all temptations.[18]

Reflection

Prayer is heart-speech with God. It is opening one's soul to a trusted Friend. Prayer is occasional and often spontaneous. Prayer permits each of us to begin anew this time again as though for the first time. Holy Spirit, thank you, for Goodness and Mercy in our lives.

Prayer

Matthew, Mark, Luke, and John,
Bless the bed that I lie on.
There are four corners to my bed,
Four angels round my head,
One to watch, and one to pray,
And two to bear my soul away.
Now I lay me down to sleep,
I pray the Lord my soul to keep.
If I should die before I wake,
I pray the Lord my soul to take.
Amen.[19]

The first written version is attributed to Sir George Wheler, 1668.

OMEGA

XI
ACCEPTANCE

Numbers 6:24–26

The Lord bless and keep thee: the Lord make his face shine upon thee, and be gracious unto thee: The Lord lift up his countenance upon thee, and give thee peace.

Hindu Upanishads

Lead me from death to life, from falsehood to truth.
Lead me from despair to hope, from fear to trust.
Lead me from hate to love, from war to peace.
Let peace fill our heart, our world, our universe.
Peace, peace, peace.

Adapted by Satish Kumar[20]

Reflection and Prayer

Dear Mother Earth,
we see that we and all our ancestors are your children.
With your patience, stability, endurance and creativity
you have nourished us and guided us through many lifetimes.
You have given birth to countless Great Beings,
Buddhas, Saints, and Bodhisattvas.
You are the great Earth, you are Terra, you are Gaia,
you are this beautiful blue planet.
You are the Earth Refreshing Bodhisattva—fragrant, cool, and kind.
We see that although we and our ancestors have made many mistakes,
You have always forgiven us.
Each time we return to you
you are ready to open your arms
And embrace us.[21]

Deer Park Monastery, for New Year 2021
Thich Nhat Hahn

XII
AUTHORITY

Matthew 7:12
All things whatsoever ye would that men should do to you, do ye even so to them.

Quaker Belief Concerning Authority

Quakers generally believe that the Divine Spirit is the ultimate authority. Terms such as the Inner Light, the Seed, Christ Within, Holy Spirit, Spirit of Truth, Guide, Inward Teacher, Great Spirit, and Divine Principle are metaphors referring to the nurturing power of the Divine within each person. Continuing Revelation comes from the Spirit and means that the Spirit's presence is without limitation. The Testimonies are spiritual insights, which come from the experience of generations of Quakers in response to the needs of the world. Generally, they have been identified as integrity, equality, simplicity, community, stewardship, and peace. Authority in a Quaker Meeting is derived from the gathered meeting. Ideally, Quakers attempt to discern God's Will in matters affecting personal and the community's spiritual health and well-being through prayer and trust others to test their leadings in the Light. A gleam of doubt is deemed healthy and denotes necessary humility. Quakers observe that no one person has a corner on the market of Truth. Quaker process requires courageous self-discipline to enjoy the freedom of seeking and finding Truth.

Reflection

Quakers are people. They make mistakes in judgment. Quakers do not always live up to the high standards they believe that good moral judgment and Gospel Order demand. The fact that Quakers have chosen to try to live their lives based on love and not based on fear is revolutionary. To live in the world and not be of the world, is a personal struggle. It is also a community struggle. Quakers admit that they need help to live according to the first two Commandments and the Golden Rule. They find benefit by seeking knowledge, wisdom, and understanding from each other, and from the world's noise, challenges and opportunities, complexities, and moments of tranquility and joy.

Prayer

We pray for spiritual health.
Yet, we are nourished by the poisons
of fear, anger, power, jealousy, envy, greed, and pride.
Guide us to heal into the Light of Redeeming Love.
Grant us strength in our inner being to resist the temptations of apathy, mistaken priorities, misplaced trust, attitudes of personal exceptionalism, and sanctimoniousness.
Grant us, to be born into that heaven of freedom, O Lord, that knows peace. Amen.

XIII

MORAL DEVELOPMENT

Micah 6:8
He hath shewed thee, O man, what is good; and what doeth the Lord require of thee, but to do justly, and to love mercy, and to walk humbly with thy God?

Kenneth Boulding, 1910–1993
The Nayler Sonnets[22]
And yet, some Thing that moves among the stars,
And holds the cosmos in a web of law,
Moves too in me: a hunger, a quick thaw
Of soul that liquefies the ancient bars,
As I, a member of creation, sing
The burning oneness binding everything.

Reflection

Moral development is the lifelong process of learning to exhibit a sense of justice, a sense of compassionate caring, and a sense that there are moral laws, such as "Do no harm," the Ten Commandments, and "Love one another," that govern personal and collective attitudes and behaviors. Conscientious Objectors to War take the position that waging war is morally reprehensible. Conscientious Objectors state that war is contrary to spiritual teachings and beliefs, and they hold to the desire to solve personal as well as international conflicts non-violently. They willingly choose to live in such a manner as to advocate for the common welfare and the eradication of inequities in their many forms. The chain of moral law that anchors the ships of state needs to be unimpeachable. To live in peace is the goal of righteous people everywhere to become ethically strong.

St. Francis of Assisi, 1181–1226

Serving

Lord, make me an instrument of our peace.
Where there is hatred, let me sow love,
Where there is injury, pardon;
Where there is doubt, faith;
Where there is despair, hope; Where there is sadness, joy.
O divine Master, Grant that I may not so much seek
To be consoled, as to console,
To be understood, as to understand,
To be loved, as to love,
For it is in giving that we receive;
It is in pardoning that we are pardoned;
It is in dying that we are born to eternal life.[23]

XIV

EVANGELIZING

Luke 9:6
So, they set out and went from village to village, proclaiming the good news and healing people everywhere.

Elizabeth G. Watson, 1917–2006

Only when we see that we are part of the totality of the planet, not a superior part with special privileges, can we work effectively to bring about an earth restored to wholeness.

Darkness is no less desirable than light. It is rather, a rich source of creativity… First there is the darkness of the earth in which the seeds wait all through the winter. Second, there is the darkness of the womb in which the young mammal grows into sufficient viability to be born and take its place on earth, as a separate being… And third, there is the darkness of night, when the garish sun has gone down and the things of earth are blotted out, and we may glimpse the vastness of the universe of which we are part…

We say that God is the Inner Light, but I want to affirm that also the Inner Darkness, and I do not mean desolation or evil, but a quiet waiting and creativity. "The darkness hideth not from thee; but the night shineth as the day; the darkness and the light are both alike to thee."[24]

Reflection

"Ursula Franklin was a Canadian physicist, pacifist, feminist and Quaker who defined peace as 'not so much the absence of war but the presence of justice… the absence of fear… a commitment to the future.' Thus, her desire for peace extended to a concern for women's rights, economic justice, and for the environment. Her pacifism and feminism were, she believed, inextricably linked—both necessary to the 'promise of a liveable future.' Asking herself the question, 'if I were accused of being a Quaker, would there be enough evidence to convict me?' she concluded that the only evidence lay in the testimony of daily decisions and personal conduct."[25]

Prayer

Spirit of Life and Love,
We pray to see the world with lucid eyes.
Eyes that transcend human limitation and nurture Truth's needs.
Eyes open to Creation's beauty and filled with restorative water.
We pray for mercy, faith, hope, and charity.
Amen.

XV

RENEWAL

Revelation 21:1, 4–5b
And I saw a new heaven and a new earth: for the first heaven and the first earth were passed away, and there was no more sea… And God shall wipe away all tears from their eyes; and there shall be no more death, neither sorrow, nor crying, neither shall there be any more pain: for the former things are passed away… Behold, I make all things new.

George Fox, 1648
Now I was come up in spirit through the flaming sword into the paradise of God. All things were new, and all the creation gave another smell unto me than before, beyond what words can utter.[26]

Carole Spencer
For early Quakers, holiness was the whole of Quakerism, personal, experiential, mystical, communal, and ethical.[27]

Reflection
Buddhist, Confucian, Christian, Hindu, Jain,
Followers of Islam, Jewish, indigenous beliefs,
People without belief…
All cry out for universal spiritual renewal
for the sake of peace on earth for all.

Prayer
Holy Spirit Divine,
Help us with our quest to be strong in faith, faithful in love,
compassionate, kind, and loving to one another.
Thy will be done. Amen.

PAX DOMINI SIT SEMPER VOBISCUM

(May the peace of the Lord be with you always.)

Afterword

The journey into faith is personal, but it does not occur in isolation. The faith journey is relational, dynamic, and ever-evolving. "Guides" are needed who encourage creative explorations, point out blind spots, and sustain communication during periods of doubt. We are led from childhood to maturity to the faith-sustaining condition of being able to access the "teacher within" with confidence. Then, as spiritual beings on a human journey, to cite Pierre Teilhard de Chardin's insight, we discover how to accept our mortality.

St. Paul wrote: *For we brought nothing into this world, and it is certain we can carry nothing out* (I Timothy 6:7). Birth and death are facts of life. Along the journey to faith, we learn to employ our gifts in the service of others. Fortified by this basic knowledge, we are liberated to overcome certain basic fears and to approach the life force as co-creative companions.

Irvin D. Yalom, M. D., wrote in *The Gift of Therapy*, "Four ultimate concerns, to my view, are highly salient to psychotherapy: death, isolation, meaning in life, and freedom."[28] The goal of mental health may be seen as co-related, even concurrent, to healthy spiritual development. The journey into faith involves addressing these fundamental fears with family, friends, colleagues, and "elders"; thus, becoming liberated as healthy human beings who also strive to be spiritually healthy traveling companions. Moral, ethical and spiritual health in body, mind, relationships, and with the Divine Spirit, is the mantra.

The great mystery of faith demonstrates spiritual discovery as personal, relational, and evolving. It shows Divine Love as immanent and transcendent. Human beings learn to see themselves as beloved and to share that experience of Divine Love with others. In becoming a person of faith, it is desirable to be a vibrant, empathetic person engaged with the community, even as one recognizes one's own fallibility. Each of us is on a conjoined journey to express love for God. We understand God and our love for each other as fellow pilgrims seeking to confirm the sacredness of Creation.

The use of the *KJV* was on purpose for its comfortable familiarity and poetic language. Also intentional was the use of *Quaker Faith and Practice for Friends (Quakers) in Britain* and the internet for their accessibility, usefulness, and near universality.

Endnotes

1. Fell, Margaret, https://quotessayings.net/authors/margaret-fell-quotes/
2. Scripture references are from the *King James Version*.
3. Penn, William (1644–1718), *Quaker Faith and Practice*, 5th edition. The book of discipline of the Yearly Meeting of the Religious Society of Friends (Quakers) in Britain, 22.95.
4. Shakespeare, William. *Hamlet* (III. i. 24–27).
5. Pennington, Isaac (1616–1679), *Quaker Faith and Practice*, 10.01.
6. Howgill, Francis (1618–1668), *Quaker Faith and Practice*, 26.71.
7. Barclay, Robert (1648–1690), *Quaker Faith and Practice*, 19.21.
8. Fox, George (1624–1691), *Quaker Faith and Practice*,16.32.
9. Shepard, Beverly, "1.92 Chapter 1: Experiencing Our Faith," *Faith and Practice, Canadian Yearly Meeting of the Religious Society of Friends*, 44.
10. John Woolman (1720–1772), Quaker Faith and Practice, 20.10.
11. The Prophet Muhammad, https://www.techofheart.com/2007/07/light-prayer-of-muhammad-last-messenger.html
12. Dewsbury, William (1621–1688), *Quaker Faith and Practice*, 19.33.
13. http://www.un.org/en/about-us/universal-declaration-of-human-rights
14. Fry, Elizabeth (1780–1845), *Quaker Faith and Practice*, 23.98.
15. A meeting of elders at Balby (1656), *Quaker Faith and Practice*, 1.01.
16. Brown, A. Barratt (1887–1947), *Quaker Faith and practice*, 27.43.
17. Watson, Elizabeth G. (1917–2006), "Ask Not Good Fortune," *Friends Journal*, May 1, 1980. https://www.friendsjournal.org/wp-content/uploads/emember/downloads/1980/HC12-50682.pdf.
18. Nayler, James (1618–1660) quoted in *There is a Spirit: The Nayler Sonnets*, by Kenneth Boulding, x.

19. Sir George Wheler (1651–1724), *The Protestant Monastery; or Christian OEconomicks, containing Directions for the Religious Conduct of a Family,* 1698. https://en.wikipedia.org/wiki/Now_I_Lay_Me_Down_to_Sleep

20. Kumar, Satish. In Ratcliffe, S. (Ed.), *Oxford Essential Quotations*. Oxford: Oxford University Press. (Retrieved 27 August 2022).

21. Thich Nhat Hahn (1926–2022), *Dear Mother Earth.* https://plumvillage.app/prayer-to-mother-earth-and-our-ancestors-new-year-2021

22. Boulding, Kenneth (1910–1983), "I. There is a Spirit which I feel," *The Nayler Sonnets*, 1.

23. Assisi, St. Francis (1181–1226). "Serving," in *The Oxford Book of Prayer* (New York: Oxford University Press), p. 75.

24. Watson, Elizabeth G. (1917–2006), "Your God is Too Small," in *Quaker Visions of Creation Restored,* 1996. https://quaker.org/legacy/quakernature/Qvisionsquotes.html

25. Franklin, Ursula (1921–2016) from *Quakers in the World: Ursula M. Franklin, 1921–2016.* https://www.quakersintheworld.org/quakers-in-action/208/Ursula-Franklin

26. Fox, George, *Quaker Faith and Practice*, 26.03.

27. Spencer, Carole (2003), "Quaker Holiness: A Response to John Punshon's Reason for Hope," *Quaker Religious Thought,* vol. 99, article 4.

28. Yalom, Irvin D., M.D., *The Gift of Therapy*, p. xvii.

Bibliography

Electronic

Anderson, Paul N. "A Tribute: Remembering John Punshon (1935–2017)." *Quaker Religious Thought*, vol. 129, article 10 (2017). https://digitalcommons.georgefox.edu/qrt/vol129/iss1/10

Boulding, Kenneth. *There is a Spirit: The Nayler Sonnets.* Nyack, NY: Fellowship Publications, 1964.

Frye, Mary E. *Do Not Stand at My Grave and Weep.* (1932). https://emilyspoetryblog.com/biography-of-mary-elizabeth-frye

Kumar, Satish. In Ratcliffe, S. (Ed.), *Oxford Essential Quotations* (Oxford: Oxford University Press).Retrieved 27 Aug. 2022, from https://www.oxfordreference.com/view/10.1093/acref/9780191826719.001.0001/q-oro-ed4-00006445

Light Prayer of Muhammad, the Last Messenger. https://www.techofheart.com/2007/07/light-prayer-of-muhammad-last-messenger.html

Spencer, Carole. "Quaker Holiness: A Response to John Punshon's Reason for Hope," *Quaker Religious Thought*, vol. 99, article 4 (2003). https://digitalcommons.georgefox.edu/qrt/vol99/iss1/4

Thich Nhat Hahn. https://plumvillage.app/prayer-to-mother-earth-and-our-ancestors-new-year-2021/

Universal Declaration of Human Rights. https://www.un.org/en/about-us/universal-declaration-of-human-rights

Ursula M. Franklin. https://www.quakersintheworld.org/quakers-in-action/208/Ursula-Franklin.

Watson, Elizabeth. "Ask Not Good Fortune," *Friends Journal*, May 1, 1980. https://www.friendsjournal.org/wp-content/uploads/emember/downloads/1980/HC12-50682.pdf

Watson, Elizabeth. "*Your God is Too Small.*" In *Quaker Visions of Creation Restored* (1996). https://quaker.org/legacy/quakernature/Qvisionsquotes.html

Wheler, Sir George. *The Protestant Monastery* (1698). https://en.wikipedia.org/wiki/Now_I_Lay_Me_Down_to_Sleep

Texts

Assisi, St. Francis. "Serving," in *The Oxford Book of Prayer*. New York: Oxford University Press, 1988.

Authorized King James Bible (KJV).

Quaker Faith and Practice, 5th ed. The Yearly Meeting of the Religious Society of Friends (Quakers) in Britain, 2013.

Shepard, Beverly. "Quaker Understanding of Christian Faith" (1.92). *Faith and Practice Canadian Yearly Meeting of the Religious Society of Friends*. Ottawa, 2011.

Trimble, Dorothy. "God, my constant companion and source of inner strength." Used by permission of Ginny Walsh, Dorothy Trimble's executor, 2022.

Yalom, Irvin D., M.D. *The Gift of Therapy*. New York: HarperPerennial, 2009.

www.ingramcontent.com/pod-product-compliance
Lightning Source LLC
Chambersburg PA
CBHW042355070526
44585CB00028B/2936